Messner Holiday Library
Easter Fun
by Judith Hoffman Corwin

Julian Messner   New York

All rights reserved including the right of
reproduction in whole or in part in any form.
Published by Julian Messner,
A Division of Simon & Schuster, Inc.
Simon & Schuster Building,
1230 Avenue of the Americas
New York, New York 10020
JULIAN MESSNER and colophon are trademarks of
Simon & Schuster, Inc.

10 9 8 7 6 5

Manufactured in the United States of America

Design by Judith Hoffman Corwin

Library of Congress Cataloging in Publication Data

Corwin, Judith Hoffman.
   Easter fun.

   (Messner holiday library)
   Includes index.
   1. Easter decorations—Juvenile literature.
2. Easter cookery—Juvenile literature.   I. Title.
II. Series.
TT900.E2C67   1984   745.594′1   84-9122
ISBN 0-671-50798-2 (lib. bdg.)
ISBN 0-671-53108-5 (pbk.)

Contents

For You

Easter is a wonderful spring holiday. Easter means the joy of celebrating the Earth's new year of growth. The sun shines brightly, flowers bloom, grass becomes green, buds and leaves appear on the trees. Birds build their nests, lay their eggs, and begin to raise their young. After the long winter, animals reappear in the woods and play freely. Many new ones will soon be born.

Easter Fun will help you enjoy Easter in a special way. It is full of ideas for making Easter baskets, decorations, presents, and good things to eat. There's even an Easter tea party! Best of all you will be able to make everything yourself, using mostly things that can be found around your home. You will also learn why we do some of the things we do at Easter time.

When you are making the projects, remember to follow the directions carefully, be patient, and most of all, enjoy yourself!

About Easter

Most countries in the world have a day to celebrate the arrival of Spring. Eastre, the Goddess of Spring, gave the Easter festival its name. Some of the customs connected with Easter go back to ancient pagan rituals. But many of them have religious meanings.

Easter, which may fall on any Sunday from March 22nd to April 25th, comes at the end of the Christian Holy Week. Holy Week stands for the last week that Jesus was on Earth. On the Sunday before Easter, Palm Sunday, Jesus walked through the palm-scattered streets among welcoming crowds. On God's Friday, or Good Friday, as we call it today, the ancient Romans put Jesus on a cross to die. Christians use the cross as a symbol of their religion because of this. On the very first Easter Sunday, friends of Jesus went to His tomb and were told by an angel that He had risen from the dead.

Throughout the world Easter is celebrated differently. Each country has a particular custom that makes its Easter celebration unique and special. Two enduring symbols of Easter are the Easter bunny and the Easter egg.

Almost everywhere that Easter is observed, eggs are an important part of the celebration. The ancient Egyptians exchanged eggs thousands of years ago. The Jewish people celebrate Passover in the spring. The egg is an important part of that festival since it is one of the special foods prepared for the Passover meal. The egg is a symbol of new life and that is why it has come to stand for the resurrection (rising up) of Jesus. It is said that the custom of egg rolling comes from the rolling away of the stone from the entrance to the tomb of Jesus.

The Easter bunny is really a hare. The ancient Egyptians believed that the hare was the symbol of the moon. The exact date that Easter is celebrated is determined by the moon. In the year 325 A.D., during the reign of the Emperor Constantine, the council of Nicaea decided that Easter should fall on the first Sunday after the first full moon following the twenty-first day of March (the beginning of spring). The hare was the favorite animal of Eastre, the spring goddess, and so the bunny has come to represent love, fertility, and growth.

Other customs and practices of Easter include wearing new clothes to celebrate the new year of life. In New York and other cities, an important part of the holiday is the Easter Parade. People stroll down Fifth Avenue in their finest and newest clothes, including the ladies' Easter bonnets! Flowers are a favorite gift at Easter, especially the Easter lily which also decorates the churches.

The sun is an important part of Easter. Without the sun there would be no life on Earth. To welcome the returning warmth of the sun, many people go to outdoor church services before dawn on Easter Day and watch the sun rise. These sunrise services are another way of celebrating spring and Easter.

Before You Begin

Make your own pattern

Directions for most of the projects in this book include patterns for you to make an exact copy of what is shown. You don't want to cut up the book, so make your own patterns with tracing paper. Begin by placing a piece of tracing paper over the pattern to be transferred from the book. Using a pencil with soft lead, trace over the outline of what is in the book. When you have finished, cut out what you have drawn on the tracing paper. Now you have your own pattern.

Using your pattern

Pin your pattern or hold it down carefully on the paper or fabric you have chosen to work with. Draw around the edges of the pattern. Then lift up the tracing paper pattern and go on with the other instructions for your project.

Materials you will need

The basic materials you need are readily available from stationery stores and art supply shops: cardboard, oaktag, heavy white paper, and colored paper. Extras like cloth and bits of lace may be found at home or at fabric departments in stores. For details or accents you'll need colored markers (waterproof), pencils, or watercolors. You will also need a sharp pair of scissors and a good brand of white glue.

Preparing a work area

Before starting to work, make sure that all your supplies are at hand and that everything is neat and clean. Cover your work surface with newspaper to protect it from glue. By the way, when you work with glue always spread a thin, even coat. A thin coat sticks better and is less likely to cause the paper to buckle.

For the cooking projects you will need an adult to help you with the stove.

Most projects in **Easter Fun** can be made quite easily. Some may prove more of a challenge—but you can do them all. Have fun!

12

Easter Sunday Late Afternoon Tea

"Come for tea" is a warm invitation that promises friendly company and delicious treats. A small tea party is always great fun to prepare and even more to enjoy. Many storybook characters have participated in such delights—Paddington Bear loved tea with jam cakes and cream. The Toad in *The Wind in the Willows* was served "a plate piled up with very hot buttered toast," and remember the famous "Mad Hatter's Tea Party" with Alice and the Mad Hatter who dunked his ticking watch into his tea?

This Easter Tea will feature four different kinds of tea, marshmallow bunnies, small finger sandwiches, Bunny Biscuits, Bunny Butter Cookies, marble swirl cake, and even strawberries dipped in chocolate. You can make boy and girl bunny tea party invitations and send them to your friends.

Boy and Girl Bunny Tea Party Invitations

These bunnies are super-easy to make.

MATERIALS:

$8\frac{1}{2} \times 11''$ piece of paper
tracing paper
pencil
scissors
colored felt tip markers

METHOD:

1. Cut the piece of paper into four equal parts.

2. Now fold each of the four papers in half along the length.

3. Trace the pattern for either the boy or girl bunny onto the tracing paper. You can make whichever one you like—or both!

4. Place the pattern onto the folded paper and hold together with one hand. With the other cut along the outline. Unfold the paper and you have a full girl (or boy) bunny!

5. With the felt tip markers draw in the bunny's features and clothes, as shown.

6. On the reverse side write the date, time, and place for your party. These bunnies can also be used for Easter cards.

Teas for Easter

Here's how to make the four different kinds of tea for your party.

INGREDIENTS:

regular tea
3 tea bags—orange pekoe tea
serve with lemon or milk and sugar

spice tea
3 tea bags—orange pekoe tea
3 lemon slices
3 cloves (one in the center of each lemon slice)
serve with sugar

cinnamon tea
3 tea bags—orange pekoe tea
$\frac{1}{2}$ teaspoon cinnamon
serve with lemon or milk and sugar

lemon tea
3 tea bags—orange pekoe tea
3 lemon slices
serve with sugar

UTENSILS:

kettle
teapot
teacups and saucers
cake plates
teaspoons
paper napkins
sugar bowl, creamer
small dish to hold lemon slices

DIRECTIONS:

1. These same directions should be used for brewing all four varieties of tea. Fill the kettle with fresh cold tap water and put it on the stove to boil.

2. While the water is boiling, prepare the teapot. Rinse it out and then fill it with hot tap water. Be sure to put the lid on the teapot to keep it warm. Empty the teapot just before you fill it again with the boiling water from the kettle.

3. Choose the type of tea that you would like to make. Put the necessary ingredients into the teapot and then pour the boiling water over them. Use enough boiling water to fill the teapot. This should easily make four cups of tea.

4. Allow the tea to brew for 3-5 minutes. Remove the teabags and serve.

Marshmallow Bunnies

These adorable bunnies are sugary sweet and quite perky-looking with their bright red bows.

INGREDIENTS:

5 marshmallows for each bunny
red gumdrop
black gumdrop
cotton ball
scraps of white paper
6″ of red ribbon, $\frac{1}{4}$″-wide

UTENSILS:

toothpicks
jellybeans
paper doily
serving dish

DIRECTIONS:

1. Use three of the marshmallows to make the bunny's head and body. Cut the other two marshmallows in half to make the four paws.

2. Keep the marshmallows together with toothpicks, checking the illustration for proper placement.

3. Cut two bunny ears out of white paper and attach them to the bunny with half a toothpick each.

4. Use the red gumdrop for the bunny's nose, attaching it with half a toothpick. Use half a black gumdrop for each of the bunny's eyes, attaching each with half a toothpick. Tie a red bow around the bunny's neck.

5. Make as many marshmallow bunnies as you like. Arrange them on a plate with a doily underneath them, surrounded by jellybeans.

Small Finger Sandwiches

Tiny sandwiches of peanut butter and honey; tuna; lettuce and tomato; and cucumber. Displayed on a platter, they look very special, and they are a great first course for afternoon tea.

INGREDIENTS:

loaf of white bread
peanut butter
honey
small can of tuna
lettuce
tomato
cucumber
mayonnaise
salt and pepper

DIRECTIONS:

1. To make the peanut butter and honey sandwich, spread the peanut butter onto one slice of bread and the honey onto another. Put the sandwich together and trim off the crust. Cut into quarters.

2. To make the tuna sandwich, drain, then mix the tuna with mayonnaise, salt and pepper to taste. Spread on one piece of bread and cover with another. Trim off the crusts, and then cut the sandwich into quarters.

3. To make the lettuce and tomato sandwich, break off one leaf from the head of lettuce. Rinse and pat dry. Slice the tomato as thin as you can and put about three slices on one piece of bread. Put the lettuce leaf on top. Spread mayonnaise on the other piece of bread and salt and pepper to taste. Trim the sandwich and cut into quarters.

4. To make the cucumber sandwich, peel half a cucumber. Slice and place in a sandwich with mayonnaise and salt and pepper. Trim the sandwich and cut into quarters.

5. You can arrange your sandwiches on a serving plate with doilies.

18

Bunny Biscuits

These biscuit bunnies are fun to make and eat. They would be wonderful to serve for breakfast on Easter morning.

INGREDIENTS:

1¾ cups presifted flour
½ teaspoon salt
3 teaspoons double-acting baking powder
6 tablespoons melted butter
¾ cup orange juice
raisins for bunnies' eyes
extra flour to dust rolling pin and counter surface
butter to grease cookie sheet
milk, to be spread onto biscuits before baking

DIRECTIONS:

1.   Turn on the oven to 350° (ask an adult for help).

2.   Combine the flour, salt, and baking powder in the large mixing bowl.

3.   Add the butter and orange juice. Mix well.

4.   Sprinkle a thin layer of flour over a work surface (a clean kitchen counter top will do). Place the dough from the mixing bowl onto the work surface and knead it about ten times with the palms of your hands.

5.   Put some flour onto a rolling pin and roll out the dough until it is about 1/2″ thick.

6.   To form the bunny, cut five pieces from the rolled-out dough as follows: one large circle 3″ wide for the body; one circle 1½″ wide for the head; another circle 1½″ wide cut in half and shaped into the ears. With the

UTENSILS:

large mixing bowl
mixing spoon
measuring cups and spoons
cookie sheet
3″ diameter circle cookie cutter
1½″ diameter circle cookie cutter

scraps of dough, form a small ball in your hand to make the tail.

7.   Assemble the bunny as shown in the illustration. Add two raisins for eyes. Place the assembled bunny on a greased cookie sheet. With your fingers, sprinkle a little milk over the bunny.

8.   Repeat steps 6 and 7 until the dough is used up. This recipe should make about six bunnies.

9.   Bake the biscuits for about 15 minutes, or until lightly browned.

Bunny Butter Cookies

These bunny cookies are delectable! A great addition to any tea party; your guests will want more and more!

INGREDIENTS:

2 cups flour
pinch of salt
1 teaspoon baking soda
1 teaspoon ground cinnamon
1½ sticks of sweet butter
½ cup sugar
1 egg yolk
2½ tablespoons corn syrup
raisins
extra butter to grease cookie sheets
4 tablespoons flour to prepare work surface

UTENSILS:

small mixing bowl
large mixing bowl
measuring spoons and cups
rolling pin
spatula, knife
cookie sheets, wax paper
platter

MATERIALS (to make bunny pattern):

pencil
scissors
tracing paper
cardboard

DIRECTIONS:

1. Turn on the oven to 350° (ask an adult for help).

2. Combine the flour, salt, baking soda, and cinnamon in the small mixing bowl.

3. Beat the butter, sugar, and egg yolk in the large mixing bowl until light and fluffy. Add the corn syrup.

4. Stir in the flour mixture. You will now have a stiff dough. Wrap this dough in wax paper and chill for several hours. If you do not want to use all the dough at once, you can leave some of the dough in the refrigerator for another day.

5. Roll the dough to $\frac{1}{4}''$ thickness on a lightly floured surface. Use a bunny-shaped cookie cutter to cut out the cookies or you may want to make your own cardboard bunny pattern around which you can cut the cookies. Use the pattern below and follow directions on page 39. If you use the cardboard pattern, place it on the rolled-out dough and cut around the outside edges with a knife. Lift the pattern and repeat.

6. After the cookies have been cut out with the pattern or stamped out with the cookie cutter, place them 1″ apart on a lightly greased cookie sheet. Use raisins to make the eyes for each bunny.

7. Bake for about 10 minutes or until the cookies are lightly browned at the edges. Remove from the cookie sheets after they have cooled for 15 minutes and place on a platter for serving.

8. If you wish, you can make a lemon icing by combining 1 cup of confectioner's sugar with about 4 teaspoons of lemon juice. Mix until smooth, add more lemon juice, if necessary, and then spread over the cookies.

pattern

Marble Swirl Cake

The rich chocolate swirls in this loaf cake give it a scrumptious taste and the dusting of confectioner's sugar makes it look quite fancy.

INGREDIENTS:

½ cup (1 stick) sweet butter, softened
1 cup granulated white sugar
2 cups sifted all-purpose flour
1 tablespoon baking powder
¾ cup milk
1 teaspoon vanilla
4 tablespoons cocoa
3 egg whites
extra butter to grease the pan
confectioner's sugar

UTENSILS:

9 × 5 × 3″ loaf pan
large mixing bowl
2 small mixing bowls
measuring cups and spoons
spatula, sifter, eggbeater, toothpick
potholders, wire rack, knife

DIRECTIONS:

1. Turn on the oven to 350° (ask an adult for help). Grease the loaf pan with the extra butter.

2. Place the butter and sugar in the large mixing bowl and beat until light and fluffy. Add the flour, baking powder, and the milk to the butter mixture; then add the vanilla and beat until smooth.

3. Remove one cup of batter and place in one of the small mixing bowls. Blend in the cocoa.

4. In the other small mixing bowl beat the egg whites with the eggbeater until they are stiff and hold a peak. Then carefully stir them into the white cake batter in the large mixing bowl. You will now have a large mixing bowl with white cake batter and a small mixing bowl with chocolate batter. Alternately spoon the white batter and the choco-late batter into the loaf pan. Mix together, making swirls in the batter with the spatula.

5. Bake for 45 minutes, or until a toothpick inserted in the center of the cake comes out dry.

6. Using potholders, remove the loaf pan from the oven. Let cool for 10 minutes in the pan. Then run a knife along all four sides of the cake to loosen it from the pan. Turn the pan upside down on a wire rack and gently tap to remove the cake. Let the cake cool completely on the wire rack before slicing. Use a sifter to lightly sprinkle the top of the cake with confectioner's sugar. Now it is ready to serve!

22

Strawberries Dipped In Chocolate

These chocolate delights look great and are a cinch to make!

INGREDIENTS:

1 pint fresh strawberries (with the stems
   still attached)
8 oz. package of semi-sweet chocolate pieces
2 tablespoons heavy cream
½ teaspoon vanilla

UTENSILS:

small and medium size saucepans or a double boiler
measuring spoons
paper towels
wax paper
dish
potholder

DIRECTIONS:

1. You will need to use a double boiler for this recipe. If you do not have one, fill a large saucepan ¼ full with cold water and put a smaller saucepan inside it. (The smaller saucepan must be just big enough to fit halfway into the bottom pot so that it rests on water.) A double boiler is necessary so that the chocolate cooks over water instead of direct heat. Otherwise, your chocolate will burn.

2. Combine all the ingredients except the strawberries in the top of the double boiler. Allow the water in the bottom of the double boiler to simmer while you stir the mixture until it is completely smooth.

3. Turn off the heat and set the small saucepan on a potholder on the kitchen counter. Holding the strawberries by their stems, dip them halfway into the chocolate.

4. After the strawberries have been dipped, place them on a sheet of wax paper. Chill and let them set for about half an hour, and then transfer them to a dish for serving.

24

Bettina and Bobby Bunny

These Easter bunnies are made from cardboard, and their new Easter outfits are made from paper, scraps of fabric, and lace. You can even string a necklace of tiny beads for Bettina. Both bunnies carry baskets and have friends to play with.

MATERIALS:

cardboard or oaktag
heavy cardboard (for the strands on which to
   place the bunnies)
tracing paper
carbon paper
white paper
bits of fabric and lace
small buttons
tiny beads
glue
scissors
pencil
felt tip markers in bright colors
black fine line felt tip marker
tape

METHOD:

1.   Place a sheet of tracing paper over Bettina, Bobby, and their clothes and trace them.

2.   Place a sheet of carbon paper over the cardboard or oaktag that you will be using to make the bunnies and their clothes. On top of the carbon paper place the tracing paper with the design on it.

3.   Gently tape the three sheets together onto your working surface at the top and bottom. This will prevent the papers from sliding around as you draw. Draw over the design on the tracing paper.

4.   Remove the tracing and carbon papers. With the black fine line felt tip marker, draw over the designs. Cut them out. Color with the other markers. Bits of lace and fabric and a string of beads can be added as you wish.

5.   Make a pattern for the stands and cut them out of heavy cardboard. Insert the bunnies in the stands.

26

Illustrated Easter Eggs

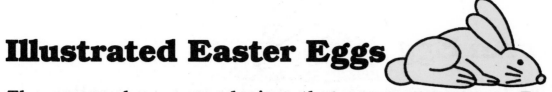

These pages have many designs that you can try on your Easter eggs. First, blow out the eggs, as described on page 30. Then draw the designs onto the eggs with a black fine line felt tip marker. Color the eggs any way you like; you can even paint them with clear nail polish to make them shiny. Each one will be an original that you can be proud of.

Blowing Out An Egg

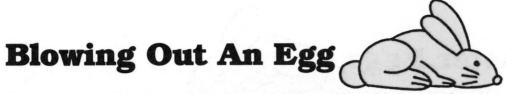

Decorating Easter eggs is great fun. If you want the eggs to last a long time, you should clean them by "blowing out" their insides.

MATERIALS:

raw eggs
darning needle
small bowl
paper towels
white glue

METHOD:

1. Holding the egg firmly but gently, with the darning needle pierce a hole in each end of the egg. Make one hole larger than the other.

2. Pass the needle through the larger hole and, breaking the yolk inside, stir the contents.

3. Blow into the small hole and force the contents out of the large hole into the bowl.

4. Clean out the egg by running a little water through the large hole. Gently shake the egg as you rinse until the egg is completely clean. If you don't do this the eggs will begin to smell after a while. Let dry on a paper towel.

5. After the egg has dried, you can put a few drops of glue over the holes to protect the egg from further cracking. Now it is ready to decorate.

Eggshell Bunnies

These little bunnies will fit nicely into your Easter basket. You can surround them with chocolate bunnies, chicks, jelly beans, and eggs that you have decorated.

MATERIALS:

3 raw eggs
3 cotton balls
scrap of white felt
black felt tip marker
scissors
white glue

METHOD:

1. Follow the directions for blowing out an egg on the opposite page.

2. With the black felt tip marker draw a bunny face on one end of each egg. At the other end glue a cotton ball for a tail. Then cut out six ears from the white felt and glue two onto each bunny. Check the illustration for placement.

3. Now the bunnies are ready for you to arrange in your Easter basket.

Bunny Inside An Egg

This charming little bunny peeks at you from inside his egg. He is easy to make out of clay for a special Easter gift.

MATERIALS:

one egg
white glue
pink, yellow, and green poster paints
paintbrush
black fine line felt tip marker
2 slices of white bread with the crust removed (day-old bread works best)
12″ square piece of aluminum foil (to mix clay on)

METHOD:

1. Prepare the eggshell into which the bunny will be placed by blowing out the contents of the egg and cleaning as described on page 30.

2. Hold the eggshell and gently chip into it until you have made a hole large enough for the bunny to fit into. Almost half the eggshell will be left.

3. To make the clay out of which the bunny will be formed, place the aluminum foil on your working surface and break up one slice of the bread into crumbs.

4. Add 1½ teaspoons of white glue and mix with the breadcrumbs, adding as many drops of water as are needed to make the mixture feel like clay.

5. When the clay has been made, form it into a lump. Wash your hands before continuing work.

6. To make the bunny, first make a large ball from the clay for the body, then a slightly smaller one for the head, and two smaller ones for "arms." Take two small strips of clay for the ears. Check the illustration for the proper sizes of these pieces.

7. Attach the head to the body by adding a tiny drop of water; repeat for the "arms."

8. Shape the two strips of clay that are to be the ears and attach them to the head with a drop of water.

9. After the bunny has been completed, gently curve the bottom so that it will fit easily into the eggshell. Test the fit by trying to place the bunny in the shell—you may have to adjust an ear or break away more shell to make him fit properly. Once you are sure that the fit is okay, remove the bunny to dry. It may take one to two days for the clay to dry.

10. Before painting, make sure that the bunny has completely dried. Paint the bunny yellow. Make two eyes with the black marker. Use the pink paint to give the bunny a nose and to color the inside of the ears.

11. When the paint has dried, glue the bunny into the egg, as shown.

12. To make a base for the egg, take the slice of bread and repeat the same procedure you did in steps 3 and 4 to make the clay for the bunny.

13. From the clay, form a little mound on which the egg is going to rest.

14. Gently press the eggshell into the mound to form a curve that will fit the egg exactly. Remove the egg to allow the base to dry. After the base has thoroughly dried, glue the egg to it, checking the illustration for proper placement.

15. Paint the base green. You can also paint some pink and yellow flowers along the bottom.

34

Easter Baskets

Lovely Easter baskets can be made from almost any small container that doesn't have printing on it and that will hold at least four eggs. A small white gift box, a green cardboard strawberry container, or a plastic tomato container will work well. An empty straw basket that your mother will allow you to borrow would also be good.

MATERIALS:

small container
colored construction paper
scraps of fabric
buttons, beads
rickrack, ribbon, lace
white glue, tape
scissors

METHOD:

1. Select the container that you are going to use for your Easter basket. Look at the illustrations on the opposite page to get some ideas on how you would like to decorate it. Use your imagination as you decorate with the fabric, buttons, beads, rickrack, ribbon, and lace.

2. Add to the decorations on your basket by cutting hearts from pink or red construction paper and gluing them on. If you have borrowed your mother's basket, instead of using glue, attach the hearts with a small piece of adhesive tape, rolled in a circle and stuck on the back of each heart.

3. You can cut daisies out of yellow construction paper and glue or tape them to the basket as well.

4. Tie bows on your basket with ribbon.

5. Cut green construction paper into thin strips to make some "grass." Make as much grass as you need to fill up the bottom of the basket to make a nice nest for your decorated Easter eggs.

6. Your Easter basket is now all ready for the eggs that you have decorated, and the jellybeans and other candy that you have collected.

36

Jellybean Sacks

These convenient little sacks are neat for holding your jellybeans.

MATERIALS:

$\frac{1}{4}$ yard unbleached muslin (this should make
  4 sacks)
1 yard of $\frac{1}{2}''$ red ribbon
pencil, ruler
scissors
tracing paper, carbon paper
tape, white glue
black fine line felt tip marker
colored markers
jellybeans

METHOD:

1.   For each jellybean sack, cut a piece of muslin 4″ wide by 8″ long. Fold the muslin in half along the 8″ side so that you have a 4″ square. The top edge, opposite the folded edge, is to be left open.

2.   To form the sack, open up the muslin again and put a small amount of glue along each of the outside edges. Close again to secure the sack.

3.   Choose the designs you want to make and trace them onto the tracing paper, as shown.

4.   Place a piece of carbon paper on the sack and tape it down gently. Now tape the traced design on top of the carbon paper.

5.   Draw over the design firmly with a pencil. Remove the tracing paper and carbon paper. Now draw over the outline of the design with the black fine line marker. Color in the rest of the design as you like.

6.   Cut an 8″ piece of ribbon for each of the sacks. Fill each sack up with jellybeans to about an inch from the top. Tie the sack with the ribbon and make a bow. Repeat this for each of the designs given.

37

38

Frederick Fuzzy Bunny

This fluffy little fellow is cuddly and soft and very lifelike.

MATERIALS:

7″ square of white oaktag
25 cotton balls
tracing paper
pencil, scissors, white glue
pink and black felt tip markers

METHOD:

1. Trace the pattern for the bunny on the tracing paper.

2. Put the tracing paper pattern on top of the square of oaktag and hold together with one hand. With the other hand, cut all around the outside edge.

3. Draw in the eye with the black marker. Draw in the nose and the inside of the ear with the pink marker. Repeat this on the other side of the bunny.

4. Glue twelve cotton balls onto each side of the bunny. Cover the entire bunny, leaving just enough space for the eyes, nose, and inside of the ears to show through. The remaining cotton ball should be glued on for the bunny's tail.

Springtime Glider

Everyone loves to fly paper gliders. Here's an amazingly simple one to make and fly!

MATERIALS:

3 plastic soda straws
$8\frac{1}{2} \times 11''$ piece of white paper
scissors, tape
red felt tip marker
paper clip

METHOD:

1. Take the three straws and tape the ends together at the top and bottom as shown in the illustration.

2. To make the wing, fold a sheet of paper in half along the 11" side.

3. Open up the paper and fold the two corners into the center crease, as shown. Cut off the extra paper along the bottom—this paper will be used to make the tail. Fold point A to point B, as shown.

4. To make the tail, take the extra paper from step 3 above and cut it in half. You will only need to use one of these pieces. Take the piece that you are going to use and fold it in quarters, as shown.

5. Insert the wing and the tail under the top straw. Tape to hold them in place, as shown. Draw a red star on each wing as decoration.

6. Insert a paper clip into the front end (nose) of the glider to complete it. Now your glider is ready for action!

Betty and Benjamin Bunny

Betty and Benjamin are softies! These bunnies will charm everyone who sees them. Each one is a pleasure to make, and they're great fun to place in an Easter basket for someone special.

MATERIALS:

½ yard unbleached muslin (this should make at least 4 bunnies)
polyester batting
white sewing thread
straight pins
needle, thread, scissors
pencil
black fine line felt tip marker
tracing paper, carbon paper
several small brushes
several colors of acrylic paint

METHOD:

1. Make a pattern for Betty and Benjamin by tracing the designs given.

2. Take the muslin and fold it in half. Pin the muslin so that it holds together and you can cut two pieces at a time. Place the pattern on top of the muslin and trace around the outline of it with a pencil. About ¼″ away from the pattern line, cut out the pattern, leaving the pins in. Remove the pattern. This will make one bunny.

3. Sew the two sides together on the pattern line, leaving a 1½″ opening for the stuffing to go through.

4. Clip the curves so that the finished bunny won't pucker.

5. Turn the bunny inside out so the rough edges are hidden. Stuff with the batting and then stitch up the opening.

6. Draw on the bunnies' features and the outlines of their clothes with the black marker. Then, with the acrylic paints, color them in as you like. Repeat for the other bunny.

page 1—Whitney Rabbit is a talented bunny. He has just decided to decorate the most beautiful egg in the world and to give it to his friend Winifred.

Whitney's Masterpiece Mini-book

You will be able to make your very own mini-book with seven drawings and a short story about Whitney, who decorates a very special Easter egg.

MATERIALS:

2 sheets of white drawing paper ($8\frac{1}{2} \times 11''$) (use paper slightly thicker than typing paper so that the drawings won't show through)

4'' square piece of the same paper (for cover drawing)

$8\frac{1}{2} \times 11''$ piece of yellow construction paper

tracing paper, carbon paper

black fine line felt tip marker

colored pencils

pencil, ruler, scissors, white glue

$4\frac{1}{2} \times 6''$ piece of fabric

METHOD:

1. To make the pages for the mini-book, fold each of the two sheets of white paper in half along the width.

2. Fold the sheet of yellow construction paper in half along the width. This will be the cover for the book. The actual finished size of the book is $5\frac{1}{2}''$ wide by $8\frac{1}{2}''$ high.

3. Open up all the folded pages, including the cover, to begin gluing the book together. Place the open cover sheet face down on the table and carefully spread a thin line of glue all along the center fold. Press the first sheet of white paper down onto the cover, making sure to line up the center folds. Now put a thin line of glue along the fold of this sheet and press the second sheet down all along the fold. Allow to dry for 15 minutes.

4. When the glue has dried, fold the book back to its $5\frac{1}{2} \times 8\frac{1}{2}''$ size with the front cover facing you.

5. To decorate the front cover, cut a $4\frac{1}{2}''$ square of fabric and glue it onto the cover. With the black felt tip marker write the title "Whitney's Masterpiece" and sign your name, as shown. Later on the cover drawing will be glued onto the fabric.

6. To decorate the back cover, cut out a heart from the remaining fabric and glue in place on the back cover.

7. The first page of your book will be the title page. On this page write "Whitney's Masterpiece," your name and the date. The other side of this page can be the dedication page. If you want to give this mini-book to

someone special, write: "This book is for . . . " or "I made this book for . . . " and the person's name.

8. After the dedication page there will be six more pages in the book; you can number these 1–6. There will be a drawing on each of these pages, and a drawing on the front cover for a total of seven drawings. You can make your own drawings or use the designs already provided. To copy these designs, cut seven pieces of tracing paper, each large enough to cover the design. Now trace the drawings onto the tracing paper.

9. Open the book to page one and place a piece of carbon paper on the page; tape it down gently. Now tape the traced drawing on top of the carbon paper, making sure to leave at least 2″ from the bottom of the illustration to the bottom of the page. This space will be used to write the story.

page 2—Whitney goes to Cindy Chicken and she says that she will give him her biggest and best Easter egg.

10. Draw over the drawing firmly with a pencil, then remove the tracing paper and carbon paper. Now draw over the outline of the drawing with the black fine line felt tip marker. Color in the drawing as you like. Repeat this for all six drawings left to do. This includes the cover drawing which should be done onto a 4″ square of paper and then centered and glued on the fabric that has already been pasted onto the front cover (see step 5 above).

11. After all the illustrations have been finished, write the story with the black fine line felt tip marker in the space left on each page.

page 3—Cindy says that she has stored this wonderful egg in a safe place in Oliver Owl's tree. Whitney Rabbit goes to collect it.

page 4—Just as he gets to the tree he sees that Cindy's dog is chasing a cat up it.

page 5—Whitney rescues the egg and returns to his house to paint his special treasure.

page 6—Winifred has invited Whitney to tea and he brings his beautiful Easter present. He has worked hard and is very proud. Winifred rewards him with a big kiss. A job well done is a delight.

THE END

Easter Kite

What fun it is to fly a kite in springtime! Here's one that can really fly. You can decorate it with a bunny, a butterfly, a bouquet or a bird.

MATERIALS:

2 large sheets of paper, 20 × 30″ (newspaper, solid color tissue, or gift wrap paper will do)

2 pieces of wood, $\frac{1}{4} \times \frac{1}{4}$″—one 18″ long, the other 27″ long

ball of string

plastic ring, 1″ diameter (such as a curtain ring)

sharp knife, scissors, pencil, glue

tracing paper, $8\frac{1}{2} \times 11$″ sheet of colored paper

3 yards of 1″-wide ribbon

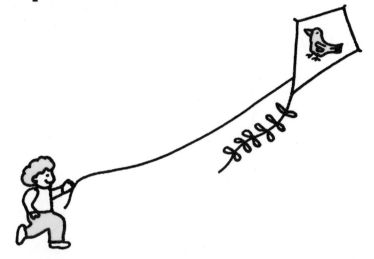

METHOD:

1. Mark with a pencil the center of the 18″ piece of wood. Make a mark 9″ from one end of the 27″ piece of wood. Matching up these marks, place the two pieces of wood into a cross shape and glue. Reinforce by winding string a few times around the cross, as shown.

2. With the knife (you may want to ask an adult to help you with this), cut a "V"-shaped notch $\frac{1}{2}$″ from each end on each of the four arms of the cross. These notches will be used to hold the string to the frame.

3. Begin to string the cross by tying string around the notch on the bottom arm, as shown. Now take the string to the right arm and knot once, then take it to the top arm, knot once; to the left arm, knot once; and back to the bottom arm, tying the end of the string to the original knot.

4. Place the kite down on one of the large sheets of paper (20 × 30″). Put a weight on the center of the cross to help hold it down. Now draw around the outline of the kite with a pencil—make your lines about 1″ out from the string. Cut the paper along the lines you have drawn.

5. Placing the kite down on the cut-out paper, cut "V" notches in the wood, 1″ deep where the arms lie, as shown. Fold and glue the paper over the string all the way around the kite. Allow to dry.

6. Now place the kite, wood side down, on the second sheet of paper and draw around the outline as you did before. Cut out the shape, and glue to the reverse side of the kite, matching edges exactly.

7. Four designs are given to decorate the kite. Choose the one you like and trace the pattern onto the tracing paper. Place the

tracing on top of a sheet of colored paper and hold together with one hand. With the other, cut the design along the outside edges.

8. Glue the design onto the kite as shown.

9. To make the kite's bridle cut a piece of string three feet long. Tie the curtain ring onto the string about one-third of the way down. Tie the bridle to the top and bottom arms of the kite, as shown. Put a drop of glue at both these places to secure the bridle.

10. Cut another piece of string six feet long for the kite's tail. Cut six pieces from the ribbon, each 5″ long. These are tied onto the tail string, one every four inches.

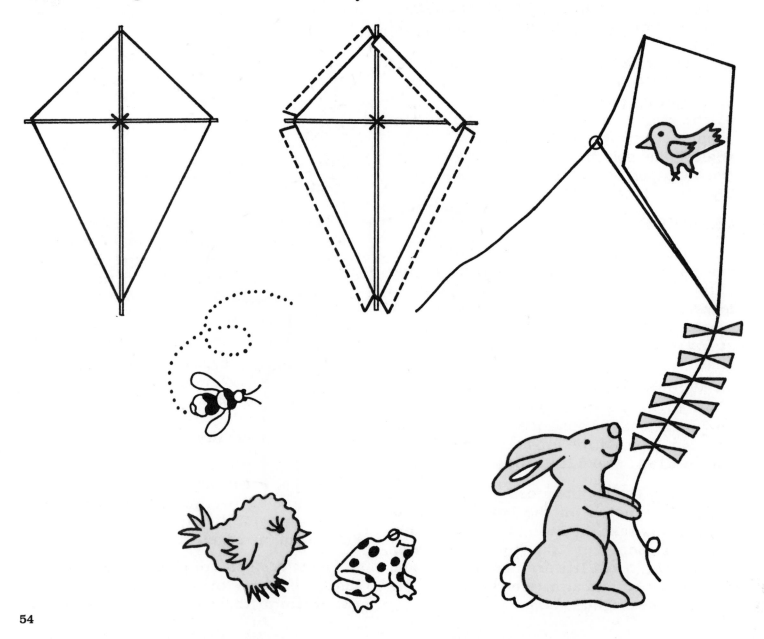

58

Pompom Bunny and Chick

White and yellow yarn can be turned into wonderful pompom bunnies and chicks. These are excellent projects to make for a school fair.

MATERIALS:

3″ square piece of stiff cardboard
white glue
scissors
pins
pencil, tracing paper
white yarn for bunny
pink felt for bunny nose
black felt for eyes (bunny and chick)
cotton ball for bunny tail
yellow yarn for chick
orange felt for chick's beak, wings, and feet
1 × 6″ piece of red ribbon
12″ long piece of red thread

METHOD:

1.   To make a pompom, hold the end of either the white (for bunny) or yellow (for chick) yarn against the cardboard with your thumb, and begin to wind the yarn around the cardboard. After you have done this several times, release your thumb and continue to wind until the cardboard is completely filled with yarn.

2.   Now carefully slip the yarn off the cardboard. Tie another piece of yarn tightly around the center.

3.   Clip the ends, top and bottom, as shown. Fluff out the pompom and shape it into a ball. Trim away any uneven pieces of yarn.

4.   For both the bunny and the chick, you will need to make two yarn pompoms. Place one pompom on top of the other and secure with a little glue. One will be the head and the other will be the body.

5.   Draw the patterns onto the tracing paper. Cut them out and pin onto the proper color felt (pink felt for the bunny, orange for the chick). Cut the felt out.

6.   Checking the illustrations for proper placement, glue the pieces of felt to the bunny and chick.

7.   The bunny's bow is made from red ribbon. First fold the ribbon in half with the ends overlapping. Wind the red thread several times around the center of the ribbon and secure it with a knot. Glue the bow into place.

Wonder-twister

These fun little twisters make the bunny look as if he has jumped right out of his top hat—or into it. Designs are also given for a flower in a basket, eggs in a basket, and a parrot in his cage.

MATERIALS:

piece of white oaktag, at least 4″ square
hole punch
compass
tracing paper, carbon paper
pencil, scissors, tape
black fine line felt tip marker
colored markers
string

METHOD:

1. Draw a 4″ circle onto the oaktag with a compass.

2. Cut out the circle and then punch two holes in it, as shown.

3. Each wonder-twister has two pictures —one on the front and one on the back of the circle—a bunny and a top hat; flowers and a basket; eggs and a basket; a parrot and a cage. Select a design and trace it onto the tracing paper.

4. Place a piece of carbon paper on the circle of oaktag and tape it down gently. Now center half of the traced design—say the bunny—on top of the carbon paper and tape it.

5. Draw over the design firmly with a pencil. Then remove the tracing paper and carbon paper. Now draw over the outline of the design with the black fine line felt tip marker.

6. Repeat steps 4 and 5 with the other drawing—the top hat—on the reverse side of the circle. It is very important to have the drawings centered on the circle exactly opposite each other so that when the wonder-twister is spun the two pictures merge together properly.

7. Color in both sides as you like with the markers.

8. Cut two 6″ pieces of string and attach one piece to each hole, securing each with a knot.

9. Now your wonder-twister is complete. Just hold the strings between your fingers and turn them rapidly, making the oaktag circle spin and merging the two pictures into one.

61

An Easter Wish

A small brown bunny
    is my friend.
He wiggles and twitches
    without end.
And I think with joy of
    the many hours I'll spend
Watching from behind
    a tree
As he romps and jumps and
    scampers with glee.
Easter is a special day
    and if I have my way
My friend will come
    so very close
That I can even kiss his nose!

Index